BLUE BUSINESS

by

GTimothy Gordon

ISBN: 978-93-6354-239-6

Printed at Repro India Ltd.

Also by GTimothy Gordon

Everything Speaking Chinese: Poems & ProsePoems

From Falling

Ground of This Blue Earth (original pub. Mellen P, NY/London)

Everything Speaking Chinese: Expanded, Revised Edition

Open House (Fictions)

Under Aries

Dream Wind

Empty

In Memory

Mr. Halbig, thanks for the memory, metaphor, meme

CONTENTS

One Art 10

Tercios del Muerte 11

Before The Fall 12

R O T H K O 13

Jackson Pollock's Talking Crude Blues 14

Summer Rhythm 15

Gas: Love Supreme 17

Willem de Kooning, **YOU** **18**

BLACK CROSS, NEW MEXICO, 1929 19

White, With Bone 20

Miró-*Imago* 22

Chagalled 23

The Business of Being Ernst 24

Hunting License 25

What Kandinsky Said 26

Klee to Kandinsky 27

Immersive 28

The Things that Grow! 29

Duchamp *Detourné* 30

Duchamp Kinetics 31

Once More to This Star 32

II

The Life	34
Nightlight	35
Sleepwalkers	36
Wake	37
Just Don't Call Me Ishmael	38
Dream Screenshot I	39
Dream Screenshot II	40
Meadowlark, Walt, Me	41
Gossamer Art	42
Summertime 2024	43
Dream of Vermeer	44
Reading the Signs	45
I *(too!)* wander'd lonely…	46
Total Eclipse	47
(Y)am Man	49
Ce n'est pas un poème sur la lumière	50
In Lux Perpetua	51
Raptured	52

III

Blue Note	54
Late	55
Too Late	56

Then	57
Private Eye	58
Cloud of Unknowing	59
Au Rebours	60
Cézanne *Saison*	61
Yo, Picasso	62
Poisson (Sans Pains), Sans du Vert, Etc.	64
As Matisse Once Knew	65
Three Crows on a Pine Bough	66
Two Crows in Winter	67
Spring-Moon	68
What We Do	69
Shop Talk	70
Tres Mújeres	72
Descend, and Sing	73
Author Bio	74
Acknowledgments	75
The Business of Blue Business	78
Photo	79

Art is the only truly effective means we have of engaging, in a communal context, the psyche on its own terms.

-J. F. Martel, *Reclaiming Art in the Age of Artifice* (2015)-

I have found my line.

-Lily Briscoe, *To the Lighthouse*-

I

Tangled Up in Blue(s)

...out of the blue and into the black
Neil Young, *My My, Hey Hey*

One Art

...something beyond themselves, beyond words.

-Paul Celan-

There's a scent that can't be defined
like breathless painting, music, dance
unplowed yet into sentient fields,
graphic grey-mists hovering water,
that won't be read or turned to tongue
but be lived in its own skin as attar
from nard or musk, commingled
jungle flora, balm from incense forests
or fetid, pressed-against-the-pavement
hog-nosed weasels littering freeway ditches,
splatters and drips reeking formidable life
without intrusive name, logic, their rank
ineffable, what we can't arrest as our own
smart and sensible and very own keepsake.

Tercios Del Muerte
(after Miles Davis)

1

The night is bait.
Stars haunt the shadows of caves.
Somewhere Miles hips
loneliness from a cone.
Measures the moon.

2

Drums fall out
of Madrid and the night
arches like Belmonte's
frozen back until there is
no more arch.

3

Plain notes to nowhere
and the wobbly stars
become a goat song.
The knife night recites *Solea*.
With cold killing control.

Before The Fall

Picasso lived this painting of tears,
blue as the humid depths of the abyss, and full of pity.
-Apollinaire-

His child's hands
keep curling, merging
moment and myth, husband,
esposa, bowed, barefoot,
shy-eyes beggaring nothing
(Nothing like the maimed
at Guernica, blind men,
sad acrobats, tumblers,
breasts nailed to nudes,
guitars the shapes of women,
tontos y locos), all crude blues,
blueboy savior blessing all
before the tide of washed blue sea,
before *duende* struck,
before the scripture, "Pablo Picasso,"
título, **LA TRAGEDIA**,
lugar, Barcelona, *España*,
that summer *surréaliste*, 1903.

ROTHKO

The reason I paint [large paintings] . . . is precisely
because I want to be very intimate and human. (1951)

I've been about my business
for over forty years
since I ditched the Coast
working the writing out
and been blind ever since
to give a name to it.
But why? They're stressed
so blue-lucid. Take **THREE REDS,**
FOUR REDS, my maroons,
my magentas— burnt all black
before my acrylics,
untitled, just numbered,
later, tattooed evacuees.
My *Spreche stimme.*
But that was long before
my cryptic Christs out West—
returning the Passion *Kaddish,*
at least.
Four blue sutures struck
three, lonely as ochre, lily,
before I finished myself,
by name,
in graphic bloodred.

Jackson Pollock's Talking Crude Blues

….fermé. A closed man.

(Matta on Pollock)

This hair-trigger poem
could have been clawed
right from Christ's clotting side,
the impasto stanched with sand
and glass and diced stones,
mica, stuck duco thrown up
or down to heaven or hell
on a wall or floor with prong,
rough brush, trowel, knife,
any fast-dancing sprung-
rhythm more or less than
critics and shrinks know,
this crude, my contours,
my *écriture*, my poles
dripping blue night.

Summer Rhythm

You are your life, nothing else.

-J. P. Sartre, *Huis Clos*-

Maybe you killed yourself, and the girl, in the process,
after all, maybe not, as you floored a '50s-finned convert
"Dreamboat" Olds up Fireplace Road, careening around, over,
the murderous Springs' curve, and speedbump, that sprawling
summer night, the girls flung sideways over the dead-drop-
down, 175 ft., a steelchromegreen chassis etched-on-flesh,
as you went hurtling through the vacant ersatz canvas top
in what must have been ecstatic freefall— in that moment
of fission, a velocity of action-art, smear of space & air
fused to the texture of stretched forms, rid of objects,
and subjects, only the night, invisible, white, the color
of Self— perfectly painterly inky sky, not a sound, or echo,
just skin naïve as wind zsst-ing through the air, and you
really fucking-A into it, now *maître*, now *métier*, under
the crushed shelves of clouds pitched onto fine Belgian
linen, Poured! this *coulage* drunk with exhaustion, late gala
at Creeks now dear without you, the scherzo skewed, your
compulsion to fly into the vortex of unframed space,
one with matter, with what *meant* something (as if anything
meant something!), the next atom of silence a flower,
peut-être, for one never liberal with love, all of this
given you, an unvarnished place to start, and stop,
an abandoned field, you who raised everything, as the night
canvas emptied out of everything, unfilling, until it was
only *grisaille*, *pleinair*, a flat, bare piece of psychic West,
Phoenix, Cody, in shadow, light, ovoid you, manchild Pip
to StellaMama, with nothing better to work than *this*,
even as the tree smacked you head-on-dead-drunk,
leaves *frisettes* strafing an imaged face not ever you,

"found" in taut night crewelwork, in blue unconscious summer,
the only line your hand or eye really knew, after all—
paint, painting, you.

Gas: Love Supreme
<u>(after John Coltrane)</u>

Riding high into the night
on John's Good Gas we shot thru
Ravenna & Rootstown & Shalers-
ville digging on Pablo Cruise &
Bob Seger & the heavy night,
but when Trane came thick on tenor
something snapped, she shifted
into low in that unknown home
where the wind peeled our heart
open to the bone.

Willem de Kooning, **You**

Willem de Kooning, **You**, sullenly mooning
your pasty brood at the Cedar Street Bar
where you first coldcocked Jack Pollock,
Cody, Wyoming-*cum*-New York, New York,
pissed at the past, and then your work posed
like hours on easels in lofts spoilt by skylights
and stain-dazed hardwoods villaged far uptown
from Queens when **ART** was blue-blooded,
back-dropted, *nouveau* fractious act all-nightly accruing
Willem de Kooning, **You**, and *poseurs*, *perdantes* all,
in trite, sudden rooms 'mid hip fits of light
New Yawk, New Yawk, *Ur*-Montauk,
that place writ in paint before bruising
your blood moon blue, Willem de Kooning, **You.**

BLACK CROSS, NEW MEXICO, 1929

Finally, a woman on paper….

-Alfred Stieglitz on O'Keeffe-

This must have been the spot out back during the Depression
on Mabel Dodge's *hacienda* off the Square, north & east,
the wooden *Calvario* banked by stones to set it straight,
fit of love, the bare sage field, saltbrush, thistles, not
a cottonwood alive, and when the sky starlit that July
she must have seen the Cross of the Brotherhood
in another light of this world, unlike men who made it,
seen without symbol, almost, flat horizontals of line,
turquoise-blue, oaken-beige, saffron, carmine, charcoalgrey
black and dense as the night fist fast closing in, now just
a sign of *Nichtung* obliterating all else, lumpy eggs about
to be hatched foregrounded, and always dead-black
straight up—**Black Cross, New Mexico**—not *gouache*, pastel,
watercolor, just smeary viscous oil, the alchemy of faith
in eye and touch and flawed geometries of space and spirit
cropped by mountain, moon, higher planes, and, as if taken
by a frank, flat sky, she must have stood back, renewed
the vision, both feet planted askew like her slack,
listless smile, lantern jaw, assumed the brushes, the oils,
palette, blunt knives, what she was called to do— painted.

White, With Bone

I have tried to paint the Bones and the Blue.

-Georgia O'Keeffe-

You snatched them clean from Outback, bleached bare, dry
by redundant desert sun, carcasses, dead and sulky all over
crimson & vermillion mesas and walled, secretive cañyons,
Houses of Mystery far removed from 5th Ave. A-Lister types
(who didn't figure, anyway), for Lord knows how long!
& stashed them in the antique black Ford until you unburied
the ghosts back at the Ranch, betook them as *Art!* in the
gristliest out-of-the-way enclaves where ghouls who found
you anyway still poach the picked-over *llano*, settling for
Sam the Shepherd's Big Pile of Bones (And Other Stuff!),
$20 & up, Española (but another totemic tale of livestock,
like **ElvisElvisElvis!** *novillados* @ La Iguana Inn up-road)—
deer & elk & antelope & horse and cattle, mainly, skulls,
pelvises, jawbones, any compostable shell without flesh
& muscle still heaped on it—in their alabaster-blasted or
ivory bone-whiteness, gutted, oblong shapes from all white
places of light, spectres imploded far back in the mind
of color, flower, ash-grey grainy adobe or reflective blue,
but mostly of spirit, staring back vacuously from dreams
so unlike live, obedient pure brute selves, geometrically
confident, hung-up-high trophies to withstand the eye
of those who sense the logic of objects, gotten the point
of *peinture-poésie*, and the like, nothing more left than
lyrical exteriors after what whirled away from unseen meat
windstonesmoothed heads & torsos & hindquarters, refilling
all holey bones, reducing anatomy to viscera, sensing what
compounds the body, vision of a thing—*Kadavergehorsamkeit*—
compliant corpora now ascending on stretchers, surfaces
gleaming in blue adobe, ghost-white callas & roses,
reclaiming sentience in cool, sanitized, tame interiors—

so like your girlish self imaged in Alfred's sepias, blacks-
and-whites, gelatin silvers, platinum pluses, each print
framed more tightly, dark hair unbound from its bun
stunning shoulders, white *chamisa* vaguely agape, one hand
maybe grazing a breast, and beyond that voluptuous mouth
and almonds for eyes what the film exposed, the woman
on paper, name never signed, recluse dotty in the desert,
savage!—. What white to know, once the eye expired,
spirit finally fled, owning those bones?

Miró-*Imago*

I will allow my instinct to guide my hand…

Without sleep for three days
and then this cabal of line,
The Dog Star craving
endless light,
blue and breathless,
out of shape in the body-night,
plunging all the way down
from fear, field-a-flush
in cock, cat, hare, snail,
gnomes with errant faces,
the fishwife baiting
Christ, the Crown,
to clear.

Chagalled

Je suis sur/Je doute

-Marc Chagall-

(Composite upon his *Crucifixion* variations, 1945-1959)

*

All that abstract color!
Disparue!
An utter *obsession*
crushed the flesh out,
left the form, the fish,
wo/man,
grooved to one
(*and only one*)
virtuoso bow.

*

Your BlueTwo!
cocked in a Christ of crowns,
jazz-sad face, gouached,
blanched a Mensch,
so gothically paled
upon two fixed sticks
(*O see*, the poet roars from Wales,
the poles are kissing as they cross),
this first, last, purpled sleep.

The Business of Being Ernst

Things are divorced from their names.

-J. P. Sartre-

A kid's dumb game, Max,
no métier for manmadness,
no less an artiste for *frottage*,
no more than your horde of color,
cardinal motley, violet-bled, pinball-blue,
eccentric as Europe kibitzed-to-bits,
Philomel deploring everyone
(*Á la tombée de la nuit, das gemeine*),
your Volk, your *Forêt Fleur*,
your seizure oneiric, Zürich gone quaintly
gaga on Dada, a *pâté*-prologue of **ART**
sprawled across your saucefleem face,
your guttural smile hatched
in a bistro beneath a trifle
cool and delectable
and *volupté*
on a plate.

Hunting License

(upon Kandinsky)

1.1   Stab a crow for good measure
1.12   Ladle the blood with care
1.13   Beware Void-like Nouns
1.14   And resolve **NOTHING**
1.15   Get back to things
       at hand
1.16   For instance
       dead matter
1.17   Conceals its own freight
1.18   Clean your sight/
       transport a snappy knife
1.19   For appearance
2.0   fold all bones
       in randy-red
       the moon Cobalt blue

What Kandinsky Said

When he splashed color
all over canvas in several arcs
and swirls, the chisel goading
a gaudy black border, up-
thrown into scalped relief,
taught to be green by the *Geist*
before *being blue being blue*
beingblue beingblue beingblue...

Klee to Kandinsky

The only thing real is the long, deep, inward gaze.
(*Diary* 20.06.1916)

The language of *Blaue*, Herr K.,
writes through me all night long
while slick ships prowl, quiet
and keeled and scrupulously
proud, and I cannot stop
waiting for morning to grant me
my great black flower!

Immersive

bluebudblueashbluesprucebluestemblueleaf
bluerosebluegrassbluefieldbluemesabluespring
blueskybluebirdbluejayblueoceanbluewhale
bluefinbluecapbluetailbluewavebluenilebluelight
bluenightbluemoonbluemoviebluenosebluelaw
bluestockingbluenunbluejeanbluedreamblueball
bluebeardbluebloodbluedevilbluegracebluegrouse
blueheelerbluebellblueberrybluesuedebluestreak
blueprintbluepencilbluelinebluebottleblue*ragout*
bluetonguebluefaceblueeyebluehairbluetoothblueice
blueblockblueribbonbluecornbluechipbluebonnet
bluestewblueflyblueblackbluedarterblueyonderblueflu
blueheartbluesuitbluecollarbluelaceblueveinblueboy
blueflamebluefunkbluemoodblueyoubluemountain
bluestonebluetbluehorizonbluebeyondbluestillness
blueairbluedreamblueflamebluespringblueleafbluebud

The Things That Grow!

(<u>upon Klee</u>)

How hills stretch,
wrench under Winter
all the way down
through SpringFall
sweet grown dreamgreen
bluefill, inheld,
from Summer!

Duchamp *Detourné*

There goes Dame Margot
whittling her toe, *plié*,
into a divot, center beam,
flanked by this stage
without walls,
luscious *demi-pointe* echoes:
The shape, our own frame,
around us, angular, airy sphere,
riveted to desire not yet felt,
geometries of dancing dreams.

Duchamp Kinetics

Is the sum of all *paroles*
whose personality
extends beyond
the floor of *this* house
and frames the angles
of notions, emptiness
of rings— is not,
Is not! the cosign of art.

Once More to This Star

(upon Marcel Duchamp)

Once more to this star
that leaves its black hole
each night and starts
straight down from heaven
to my heartsick dark pearl
never knowing where this shining
will lead the way love would
played out over undreamt streets—
this black-burning urge.

II

Kind of Blue(s)

But what is it that light cannot transfigure into beauty?
-George Eliot/Mary Ann Evans-
(IIfracombe, North Devon, UK)

The Life

After midnight, quick-gangsta-kill,
screeching, whining, hyena-like,
but not, coyote efficient, a minute,
two at most, eerie desert quiet.

Imagine the moon, were it full,
black-stain-vic-glow in the black
crusting, clotting tender white flesh,
the perps' thin, bloody lips, loping

into the outback, then reimagine her,
all the lucid stars, igniting the feast,
the commune, artless, florid faces
gnawing, tearing, wrenching, the kill,

the life, almost like falling in love.

Nightlight

Let me wipe it first, it smells of mortality.

Lear to Gloucester, who asks to kiss his hand.

-IV:6-

Step outside under nightlight,
count the stars, if possible,
not by number, name, nobody can,
except maybe the boss,
know them by glow, celestial order,
distance from earthly toehold
in this afterworld where you linger
enrapt in the moment with nothing
to hold you here but actual or artful
starlit clarity, guess why they're here
if not for you, if not for you, for who else then?
their gravity lightening heart-heavy you,
alone, sad, cloaked with guilt and shame,
darkness, dread, despair, this mortal coil.

Sleepwalkers

I wake and feel the fell of dark…

-G. M. Hopkins-

<u>April 2024</u>

Ever a fresh, dark spring wind,
late afternoon critical mass menacing
mountain col or crevice with storm
and stress bluster-gust come to nought.
We feel its full blow up-and-downhill
on- or -off street, in devil dust, pigweed whorl,
pigeon molt, rat scat drop, each dog walker,
jogger, EZ-bike peddler, wheelchair bound
lame and halt mall refugee out for sun, maybe more,
ritual a faith, of sorts, like waking nightly on cue
into predawn dark, closing with the stars' ignition,
blood orange moon heft, half or quarter slice,
stirred from second-self sleep not to dawn,
or day, just wind-waking dark spring swell.

Wake

I wake blindly in the dark
for the fourth or fifth time
hoping to hit the bowl, no yips
this time, florescence a white
macula mote, low- and -highbeam
road light day or worrying night drive,
solar bulb, coal-black lamppost standard,
iPhone mini face, fridge freezer 25-watt,
microwave, oven, iris-eye, faint desert haze
daybreak. Small blue hours' wake, Ambien,
Elavil, plastic *Fireball* 66-proof, or two,
zap me out and up before spring light
floods workroom without grit, grace,
wit, hoping for better mañana before
grinding strong, earthy, Arabica beans,
scooping them into the *Keurig*, setting
the timer, flicking on/off/pause switch,
awaiting its glow to go blue, black, blank,
even before relentless Mourning dove drone.

Just Don't Call Me Ishmael

I'm beyond knowing the Big Picture,
Art, my betters do, just never finicky
raven pivoting for any hot, bloody mess,
geese gone suddenly summer north,
grubworm, copperhead, about Outback business,
without notice or care, moonlight shine,
shimmer over desert mountain tarn,
restive, swollen night cumuli, dawn-burst,
no White Whale, odd, obsessive boss,
life-altering quest, deathless smart mate,
just curious, like them, about timeless things
of this world, artless in their living way,
book-learning gone awry.

Dream Screenshot I

At the far clump
of city desert
one pigweed shot up
for the kid
who stopped,
stooped,
knelt,
kissed,
blessed.

Dream Screenshot II

Dawn-spring-rain,
dream-green-glow

Wrinkled, mottled
leaf

Somber dove,
dank habit loosed
quill by quill

Pock-marked
desert sand,
pitted petroglyph

Heaven-sent earthsmell,
musky

Spring
aching to break
into being

Meadowlark, Walt, Me

Meadowlark sunning himself
on new high-end hacienda digs
cupola away from barrel cacti
and cottonwood, solitary, hermetic,
not many here of his kind, desert-savvy,
restless, saluting dawn in clear, sharp notes
until full light, the go-by patter turn achy,
warbly and gushy, dead-on dreamy I know,
and I know he's not just musing to dawn,
would-be few mates, just to himself,
content with his own song, voice,
I like to think, sounding very much mine,
Walt's, of absent lover, significant other,
life partner, hanging out, lonely corner cowboy
waiting for that girl in the flatbed Ford
trolling Outback edge a second, third, time
for a closer look at him, our old Walt, me.

Gossamer Art

Pale Endymion moon
ghosting desert, *echt* busker
craving attention, love,
mortal form,
poem, paint, pot or vase,
gravitas of solid sculpture,
on this kind of night,
cusp of crisp spring,
let it lie high first in music
of the spheres, faint note within
lovers who hear, see, feel,
dreaming gossamer into art.

Summertime 2024

Dawn stillness before day opens
wholly into searing white light,
heat that lays on as a weight,
stirring nothing, not even unshorn,
bleached, overflowing palms girding
our camp, except maybe small birds
flitting for scraps, dry gulch water,
yet even they stay close to shadow,
shade home, among rabbitbrush,
bull grass, squat cottonwood
(no Gershwin/Monet moment),
under wraps until winter solstice,
if then, like all desert brethren,
brute and fowl, seen or not, drawn
to dusk, dark, cold, soundless night light.

Dream of Vermeer

There are stars pinned
to bone-black night

hovering above, the hand
guided by brush, maulstick,

for once, no window blaze,
below, beneath our feet,

bottom of rock-solid earth
caught mostly in shadow,

umber, ochre, tint of graphite grey.

Reading the Signs

Most know them as omens,
fair or foul, even before having met,
embrace as lovers along the way,
never me, even after seen, and read,
assiduously, far way ahead, saw horses,
reflective rail roadblocks, dry and wet
trenchant sandbags, flashing caution
or red lights, out here, far from city, lover,
friend, home, barrier-free, doing business
with star- and -moonlight bone-dry desert,
hot, hazy air, slitherers' burrowed hideouts,
large and small fry paw- and -footprint,
flyover corbie emissions, nothing to amuse,
covet, distort, distract from things themselves,
realty-free crossbar placards, property **Posted**s,
barbed wire grated and gated fencing, no need
for signage, good thing too, June's still rockin'
my heart upon all-too-familiar scorched-earth summer
settling in my bones, plunged as far down deep
into marrow as it can get, then even deeper,
into the all of me.

I (*too!*) wander'd lonely…

The wind seized our breath.

-Dorothy Wordsworth, *Journal*, 15 April 1802-

Maybe it was just a dream
shot through with a shock
of white light across the bay,
its banks filled up with flowers,
rooted as Antaeus in Grasmere marrow
as overhead opened soundly, wondrous flashes,
and *W*, all the while, apart, like most men,
I s'pose, he took it all in, afterward, as usual,
after the many suppers with Hunt, STC, Southy,
lesser lights, many months, years later,
after peeking through my keepsake
for another way in to feel my musings
on the banks (neglecting *my storm!*),
his words Mummer-strutting page,
folio, or quarto, or octavo,
it never mattered much,
like us, but once, twice,
busting a lively move
on less staid Lake occasions,
before came Wedded Bliss,
came Great and Grumpy
and sometimes Downright Dour,
thence Lordly when leaves lost luster,
grew stale, trumpet and ruff,
like The Age, for most, and later,
tho' *I* recall exactly how *it* came
as it comes now, plagued by wind
blown up quite before the storm,

measured us mortals unseasonably,
perverting our shouldering parasols,
bore our breath, us both, clear away.

Total Eclipse

<u>April 08-12.2024</u>

Rising frisky April moon
calls to mind past loves,
mostly forgotten,
though not flame-haired Barb
(*her I remember!*)
holding my hand
each school day
on the **B** bus while I read
Gibran's sheer white
slim hardback *Prophet*,
or his other, lesser,
stacked in my bedroom,
who told me not one,
but two, filthy jokes,
a French lady, liquor,
I didn't get at all,
mostly don't now
in my semi-dotage
more involved with
day's deep darkening
total eclipse
than my lame love groove,
now memory
in ecstatic freefall

(Y)am Man

Who knows but that on lower frequencies, I speak for you?

-R. Ellison, *Invisible Man-*

-Popeye the Sailor Man, "I yam what I yam," 1933 cartoon-

Back in again from Out There where nothing lives but brute
critter & fowl, crawlies close to earth, fetid, rank
vegetation, acres of baked silica and stone and mesa,
dry gulch, arroyo, mountain, yet wild and alive, agelessly
young in unlovely, though not unloved, withdrawal, offering
nothing but subtly fresh, spikey, misshapen selves to eye,
& air, unstinting sun & wind, where time melts, as if it
never left its burn. Email, text, from schoolmates,
some close, most not, wanting to catch up, hook-up, *know me*,
assuming I'm that *that me*, I suppose, which gives pause
if past *is* past, or not, imprimaturs Aristotle-Freud-
Faulkner promulge as tragic family fiat, all I know
for sure I'm here now, beamed-up back up into cyberspace,
into boyhood, codes, hi-tech wiring, AI stuff I know
nothing about, as though back at the hop, Cottman Ave.
Burger & Malt Shoppe, Joanie's, Friday?, as if I never left
who I was, online snaps current enough to satisfy any nosy
Parker who now live airily on IG, X, Facebook, Snapchat
or Tik Tok, Tinder, Bumble, Grindr, no techie me, I never
answer (*Word*, not cool), in decadent aughts *patois du jour*,
never OG retweet, slide into DMs, mentor guilty schoolboy
habit, let past have me its own, as I was, maybe still am,
¿quién sabe?, and so sophomorically (*my bad!*), make it an
in-your-face Wilt/Dr. J. slam dunk, be like Air Mike,
ghost them all.

Ce n'est pas un poème sur la lumière

-All that glisters is not gold—-

The Merchant of Venice, II:7.73.

Out again in force, fairy lights, flinders,
tea lamps tucked-up into pitch-black,
field guide to onset fall, and more *more*,
darkness for shadow-world outliers, dreamers,
poets, brothers and sisters, all earthly others,
whatever stripe, despite wishes wished upon…
as with art, fable, myth, faint transient twinkles,
nothing in themselves, soon-to-be-burnouts,
like us, yet all things magical, mindful,
even if poems score no one nourishing meals,
stability for unsure boggy ground beneath us,
succor for life's iteral discontents, seasonal pivots,
betrayals, maudlin three-arc life highs and lows,
untimely, short-shelf, three-score-and-twenty
starts-and-stops full panoply starlight, or not,
stuff dreams are made on before daybreak,
jingle-jangle dawn, morning, bright, busy,
all-too-real-high-noon prose envelop you.

In Lux Perpetua

Early Harvest, Mooncake moon, deadnamed,
demyth*ed*, neutered, since woked *SuperBlue*,
stars too swollen like desert heat before dawn
up and down Sonoma Ranch to Golf, past Coyote
Ridge and El Segundo Trail, *The Grille* at Sunset,
putting green sward, driving range, climbing higher
into Palm Canyon and Cave Creek, between which
slipknot gap white flows way west to the Coast, Sea,
as Asian-greige smog and once secret realms already
tomorrow, stuff dreams were once made on to claim
the not-then-heavenly-known paving our autumn's,
or any other season's nights,' way, whether full-ripe,
halved or quartered, in the mind's eye, all-at-once,
Moon, in plainspeak, metaphor, meme, everywhere.

Raptured

<u>September 2024</u>

Night flyers shocked from trees,
wing-leathery flapping across first fall,
late summer, moon, caught between
earth and ripe blue light, midair vagrants
on the lam, hightailing it somewhere,
but where? bracing themselves in the joyful
all-at-once in-betweenness of everything
known, and not, neither here nor there,
steadying themselves in the aftertlight,
whatever otherworld lay beyond tree,
blue moonlight, before dreaming
how to live in it.

III

Rhapsody in Blue(s)

Plane it straight, smooth, and free from twist!

-Mr. Halbig, 8th-grade woodshop teacher chalkboard mantra-

Blue Note

My doctor wants me to give up singing ….
But what else am I made for?

-Billie Holiday-

Despite the smack and snow, booze, endless smoke,
lines in bathrooms, bedrooms, dayrooms, *to kick them blues,*
there were "overtones," what 'Trane sought, offworld
beyond notes even by spring '59 when waifish, boney,
stock-still before the mike black-clad jive hipsters
sometimes caught a whiff of, or thought they did,
where your riff went, wanted to go, downtown squares *not,*
cork-tipped Viceroys, clichéd Scotch & waters, reefer lite
highs at uptown white & grey bars, about bad, broken, love,
no matter gender, nothing new, except the flat, spare,
sober notes free and fluid, unvarnished and at 44 hoarse
and gritty *inheld* at end while alone up front, one white
gardenia stashed in Dixie Peach pomade-slick ponytail,
sexless sleeved dress cloaking tracks, set over without
bravado, gesture, groove gifted Frankie Boy, *Bend them!,*
emotion bespeaking self, no hubris, copped attitude,
scant applause receipt, just maintaining bare bones life
and art between busts until you finished that haunted
& bitter crop closing even suburban lounge gigs A&R suits
never wanted sung, backstage, Gilby's Dry 'n juice,
unfiltered Pall Mall reds, hoping some got it, that you
got away again clean.

Late

<u>(3, after Edward Hopper)</u>

1

You know it's late
the way a place looks
when you come the other way.
You can never quite wipe
the fog from your eyes,
indict the right failure.
A little like finding
your pulse fast asleep, soon.
Then, you remember your hands.
How they spoke fondly
of the place they left.
How they will feel the next time
they leave for a long spell.

Too Late

2

The sorrow men have come
and gone and soiled the night.
Their trench coats loitered like
Alan Ladd boarding **L'Express**
for Zürich. Except, of course,
they were not wan, blonde, wavery.
Nor did their footsteps measure
the roots of hours. Nor were *Straßen*
cobbly and dank, greased by spatting rain.
Only the blind by the bridge
with maps for faces
saw what we might,
and spoke
in broad, black, strokes—
too late.

3

After the long haul you wait
for the slow still-life to matter.
The door clears out like mesa, prairie,
final, undone. What's left—
Druid embroidery by design.
Nothing Moody. Dusky. Bluesy. Mauve.
Nothing to set pewter upon.
Nothing with indigo in it.
You wait. You wait for the tramps
to traipse in from the fields
braiding their raw, crotchety hats.
You brace for their brush by the door.
Then. Then you air everything.
Then the business begins.

Private Eye

Monet is only an eye. But what an eye!

-Cézanne-

How can you not adore exquisite eye candy
excess splashed over gardens, lilies of all hue,
ponds, rivers, the Seine, poplars, haystacks,
what's before the eye and sense each moment,
and what's behind bucolic farm, field, the poor
and privileged, transmuted by instinct and pigment
in audacious subtlety, more than meets the eye,
probing Nature's quiddity, watchful waiting dawn-
to-dusk shadow and light past, passing, or to come
before gone, restoring garden myth, days of heaven,
lunches on *l'herbe*, genteel ladies, book in-hand, abutting
leafy green shadowy elms, swathed head-to-foot-white,
wisp of bundled snood, Camille flaunting spring parasols
strolling with child flushed red poppy fields, among quaint
Giverny gardens, lilies, hedgerows, pastoral images dreamt
by sweatshop girls at redundant machines, newsies hawking
endless street copy, light failing them, bourgeois us,
brave new world sharp urban edges chronicling moment,
movement, absolute time by laboring clock, not elements,
sun, moon, star, beguiling fog and mist, sun and storm,
etched with immanent insight, one's self's intuitive sense
of each moment *seized* aflash, élan vital now unromantic
ends when the art line changed, cubists, constructionists,
surrealists, washed-out plein air colorists, abstractionists,
divvying-up, shriving, Nature's carcass while aged,
half-blind, depressive, L'Orangerie *Water Lilies* heft
bloomed anew! girth, breadth, depth, cold eye cast at end
on life! in color! for the rest of us.

Cloud of Unknowing

(upon Van Gogh's *Wheatfield with Crows*, 1890)

…look upon yourself as an exile and a pilgrim on this earth.

-Thomas à Kempis-

I can still see them all bent with the wheat
and wind, thick-dark heaven, full ripe tall and tawny
deep summer shocks, unshorn ears, rough swathes
of journey's end road, green, brown patches slicing
what's half-seen, what's not, all-of-a-heap palette
more full-fall Parisian than mad Arles July light,
birds of blackness, blackbirds, ravens, citron-straw wheat,
wind, unruly pulse of the spheres, field shot through
with life and light and fear and darker ends days away.

Au Rebours

What is wrought in sorrow lives for all time.

-Vincent Van Gogh-

Once out of Arles, spring and summer ins-and-outs
of Rémy, Auvers, asylums, darkness setting in before forty
beside your dreamer's disease, beloved blond wheatfields
awaiting thick oils just a shot away since brushed bronze,
crisped russet (your own Dutch color), scorched by late July
among corded, strapped haystacks, all late visions ominous,
turbulent skies (you wrote Theo), canvas fraught with serious
black crows, windswept stalks, looming squall, no razor now,
no Gauguin, just you, pistol, straight from Ibsen, Strindberg,
dénouement, gullet, spleen, not the temple, nothing dramatic
about dying asylum days later, no one beside Theo, doctor,
summer's lease cut short, head and heart pain, Van Gogh,
gone.

Cézanne *Saison*

…the father of us all…

-Monet *et* Picasso-

The art dynamic, tight, taut, fraught
when you found your line as with Émile,
Hortense, Papa, *Le Salon Paris*, early and late
booboisie who never got you, or it, the shape
of things to come, geometry pre-Picasso,
color felt *and* seen, the sense of objects in
nature and artifice, the diurnal caught in each
fresh brushstroke moment from crude, brusque,
palette-knifed, slabbed-on thick-dark skulls,
couillarde artwork, *they said*, until the primaries
took hold, enhanced still-life color, overlaid
potbellied pears, peaches, apples, melons,
blurring perspective, form, each imaged moment
on dishes, in bowls, splayed over oilskin tables,
and other stuff the *connaisseurs* finally got, albeit late,
the felt new world sensed now by Pablo, not Paul,
since *mort*, La France desecrated *again*!, some Spaniard,
outlier *métèique*, exploding, reshaping, *Now*, vision
already poised at the easel, the place of all our being
before one war, a next, when all the old color bled out.

Yo, Picasso

The highest walls melt before me.

-Picasso, self-portrait photo caption, summer 1901-

Consider me at 20 in-heat, like Paris, black cloak, black hair,
black beard, black eyes, the aughts, sans francs, friends,
tongue, full of myself, dream and vision to expiate among
othered Other misérables in Montmartre, Montparnasse, known
from high hovel-*atelier* with Braque, *notre avenir dans l'air*
gone-bust, so solo I'd show the clucks what's what, set
this century on fire, deflate a past still preening, all-in
with my genius before the lean-in, copycat, cool-kid *isms,*
consider my hands (so Stein says), delicate, of a pianist,
shape-shifter among splodgy French bric-a-brac art spooked
by all that's New and Now from the get-go by gendarmes,
government, for talking la langue of art, *a mí,* alien, *métèque,*
never *artiste,* never métier, *never citizen,* surveilled, spied on
by lowlife snitches, given the French bureaucratic go-by
time and again, despite my cosseted blues, rosés that crush
the canvas, often your heart, not just *La Vie, Les Demoiselles,*
Weeping Woman, Child with Dove, Saltimbanques, all Blind
Minotaurs, *The Tragedy, Guernica,* rejected by higher-ups,
especially my spot-on angles more avant than Armory garde
nudes descending, blues and toilets, when all went surréaliste,
after me, Dali céléb, postwar Yank abstractionist pretenders,
thugs really, boozing it up in Bowery bars, but me, my mythic
feel even brutalist touches, working overtime on what I was
before becoming the *I Am* every moment, the dealers, collectors,
money guys, who knew passion & genius, always my worth,
cash-money awash as I negotiated both wars, Olga and I
hobnobbing upscale Danse Russe artistes in pricey flats,
châteaux, trolling *le pays,* luxe Hispano-Suiza limo, fresh

mistress in-hand, partying with Dominguín after the bulls,
even before Papá H! remaking a smug, certain world, seeing it
still accessible, mysterious, just when everyone thought all
was stable, safe, and absolute for a bit before each calamity,
until The Bomb, then deeper-in mining my god instinct,
creation *en-soi*, & what a joy working, still is, at what's,
even past ninety, in flux, for what else is there, rich, poor,
young, old, scholar, scamp, but find oneself in the moment
as at Gósol when all went dark with vision & voice, the who
you know you are, meant to be, ever seek, even a microsecond
before passing, *the what* I'm after, my very being, *Yo soy,*
sin arrogancia, ahora y por siempre, más grande que la vida,
Yo, *Picasso.*

Poissons (Sans Pains), Sans Du Vert, Etc.

(upon Picasso's *Night Fishing in Antibes*, 1939)

After Picasso, there is only God.

-Dora Maar, lover/activist-photographer/documentarian-

Last time there, old men still casting splayed nets,
tho' of course, *Maître* long-war-gone to Paris, Code Red,
yet all *matériel, accoutrement*, midsummer-thick-heat,
blackout night, requisite few faint stars, rickety boats,
dramatic sea, locals bearing lamps, speared fish, no new
mistress greening, complicating lamplit effect, nor hand,
oil, vision redrawing what light inheres in mortal life,
reminding us of radiance ever artful, inheld at nightfall,
time after exquisite dark time.

As Matisse Once Knew

C'est tout space et couleur!

Love, it begins, is a space
waiting for something to share

as morning happens, and happens,
upon plain dark earth and hill,

willing its birth-hour of light, or,
fresh pears drawing evening sun,

without words, without sight, first tracking
the scent, then touching the body beside them,

never daring to move until they turn
perfectly blue. As Matisse once knew,

probably not thinking of love:
Color! It's everything!

Three Crows on a Pine Bough

(upon Buson's inkbrush painting)

Late fall parched mustard wheat
modest as a Norse king, no *risqué*
bluebell, poppy, scarlet paintbrush,
or even *outré* desert aspen, bronze turning
among mangroves of sand speckling this end
of earth, not Kyoto, in fall, the blackest of ravens,
goblins, trolling from husks of stumps bone-dry things,
all for the scent of blossom, sight of bloom,
every prickly Joshua beseeching heaven.

Two Crows in Winter

(upon Buson's inkbrush painting)

Top-heavy with snow
this branch will not break
even after darkness, blight, rain
day and night, every thin limb
seasoned ice-white,
barely a leg to stand on,
shriving color and form and light
from farm and field—*"Winter"*—
this tonsured lay monk.

Spring-Moon

Lotuses on a Summer's Evening

<u>(upon Yung Shou-p'ing)</u>

What if they're not as sublime as baroque Blue Nile lotus,
Crème-white Madonna lily, ascending aflash from sacred waters,
stems stiff as righteous Jamaican spliffs, *têtes* regally coiffured,
but just gangly and beige and somewhat scumbled, brushed on
mulberry bark or rice paper, their taupe, misty palette *Home*,
opening nightly up from rushes and shallows for no one but
themselves, Art, Nature, Poetry, and the unseen Spring-Moon
illuminating mist just enough for feel, just as it illumines
every mortal thing in this world, however briefly, fabled
glam aesthetes sporting *toque-blanche-et-azure* crowns,
milkweed and toadstool—, as sunflowers caught furiously
yellow on canvas in the act of being nothing more lovely
than already *were, are, ever have been*, in bleak, wintry Arles.

What We Do

...there is no there "There."

-Gertrude Stein-

The moon is Swiss-cheese sexy. Or black. Or peacock-blue ink.
Peut-être pink. If you're French. Whatever pricks your fancy.
If you have one. This October full-figured pastel, moon of
many colors, fat tie-dyed, stone-gas-hip throwback to, *like*,
the in-your-face '60s-'70s, coked-up crystal '80s, Don Cornelius
keeping it LA chill, deep bass downlow, unlike mystic-green
Asian harvest moons that steal upon you in the rye, sensuously,
Chang'e Virgin, Jade Rabbit, Toad, either way, east or west,
blueblood auras tight as catgut, fractious and flirtatious as
great poetry, great love, beyond bone, impressed in marrow,
blackest of black arts, tangible, brute *There* like all solid
objects *not there* some quicken, conflate, invariably color.
Of those who muddy Nietzsche's clear, sober water.
What we do.

Shoptalk

In the massive heat, the fledgling wooden scaffolding, beginning
of Sign, near where *tai-tais* do daily brunch at slick-new prefab
Biéshù expressos, hoisted tapered bamboo logs from Hsitou
Forest snapped at tight, right angles, balanced on rough-rounded
ash & ebony woods up and across touting golf course, condo,
Imperial Pleasure Dome, anything warm—green-jade-and-gold,
not just Island-hot Chinese, the woods in threes for support—
jutbraced, jerry-rigged pinwheel, baling-wire wound-round
with fire-tempered Craftsman pliers, *By Sears!*–, corralled,
clamped, clasped, hugged chest-tight by pairs of flannelled
arms before being laced & tamped justly right around soft,
curved beams with gloved peen hammers, all measured by hand,
by feel, nice sense of where things are, ought to be, in place
for right support, *materièl* winched out of trucks, threaded up
hand and shoulder through unfinished space where design,
latticework, if any wrought, might be, transparent guidewires
strung like temple Ghost Month smoking joss-sticks all across
East Asia Street, back-beam **V** supports tethered and wedged
down invisibly, sensibly, into bare hard rocks in place that
say, *this is and no other!* gangly shape set taut and upright
before rump dawn & mountain forest spirit fog from which
it comes-to-be, never-to-return, rook and magpie jawboning
morning above high-beam-and-horn AM traffic, sugarcane
spiking fields of whiplash lizards crisscrossing Misty Peak
and Pear Mountain over eastern Island Pacific meadows,
if you could see them, lapsed wind, dispossessed of breath,
a breathless caprice in the face above the balance-beam
precipice, and still it stands, even at hot equatorial dusk,
the structure, crude readymade, thing-not-yet-named,
écriture pleinair, as if taken by great stillness, & sky,
worked back through first beginnings, summer twilights,

rushes of early & late darkness, full-ripe fall moons,
black-ice nights, all evenings of all stars candling skylight
nights refining this sheer work of earth & sea & sky
planned & planed, as any made thing, deaf, dumb, & blind
old man Halbig always scrawled for us across our 8th-grade
Wednesday woodshop chalkboard—*Plane it straight, smooth,
free from twist!*

Tres Mújeres

(for Amy Clampitt and Georgia O'Keeffe)

One braiding, then drying, red chile
under grazing mesa sun, another at the loom,
eye-deep into speckled mountain, a third,
walled inside the dark adobe casa,
an eagle in aerie, with turquoise eyes,
bearing blue light from the other side.

Descend, and Sing

By river's edge, first frost,
episcopal cranes
grooming in the reeds,
and the poets in Snow Mountain,
under falling needles and leaves,
chanting their lives, without bones,
for Li-Sung's court below when they must,
like all immortals with silk-white wings,
descend, and sing.

Author Bio

Gordon holds degrees in Literature and Philosophy, Creative Writing, a doctorate in Comparative Languages and Literatures, awarded NEA and NEH Fellowships for teaching and scholarship, artist residencies, poetry prizes, and presentations of critical and creative papers in juried journals and readings at global symposia. *EVERYTHING SPEAKING CHINESE* received RiverStone Press Poetry Prize, *NIGHT COMPANY* nominated for NEA Western States' Book Awards, and Pushcarts and Best of the Net. Recognized in Poets & Writers, Inc. (NY), Maine Society of Poets, Ohio Writers' Directory, he divides lives among the borderland New Mexico/Texas Chihuahuan Desert Southwest Organ Mountains, Asia, and Europe.

Acknowledgments

A number of poems have appeared previously in journals, or shall, occasionally in unedited form, to whose editors I hereby acknowledge. All poems ©GTimothy Gordon.

"Three Crows on a Pine Bough" and "Two Crows in Winter." *The Provo Review* (2015). "Two
   Crows . . .". Rpt. *Plum Tress Tavern Journal* (2020).

"After the Fall" and "Spring-Moon." *The Scarlet Leaf Review* (2016).

"One Art." *Luminous Review* (Fall 2016). Rpt. *Rougarou: Journal of Arts and*

Literatures (2020).

"The Things that Grow." *Ekphrastic Review* (2016).

"What We Do." *Abstract: Contemporary Expressions* (Winter 2019).

"Late." *Kimera: Journal of Fine Writing* Vol. 6 (2004).

"*Tercios del Muerte.*" *The Remington Review.* Vol. 2. 1974.

"*Shoptalk.*" *Utah Foreign Language Review.* Vol. 9 (2004). Rpt. *The Pittsburgh Quarterly.* Vol. 10 (Fall
   2017).

"**R O T H K O**." *The New York Quarterly.* Vol. 63 (Fall-Winter 2007).

"Descend, and Sing." *Dimsum: Asia's Literary Journal.* Vol 11 (2005). Hong Kong, PRC.

"Late," "Jackson Pollock's Talking Crude Blues," and "The Business of Being Ernst." *Poetry Salzbörg*
   Vol. 8 (2015). University of Salzbörg Press. Austria.

"Willem de Kooning, **YOU**," and "Duchamp Kinetics." *Art and Academe: Journal for the Humanities*
   and Sciences in the Education of Artists. Vol. 11.2 (1999). New York.

"Summer Rhythm." *The Maverick Press*. Anthology 2011. Visual Arts Press, Texas. Pushcart nominee.

"Cloud of Unknowing." *Maximus Magazine* Vol. 1. Spring 2022); rpt. *Hole in the Head Review*. Vol. 3.2.
   2022.

"*Poissons (Sans Pains), Avec Du Vert, Etc.*" *Litbreak Magazine*. July 2022.

"Cézanne *Saison*." *Last Stanza Poetry Journal*. Vol 14 (Fall 2023).

"Hunting License." *The Odd Magazine*. Vol. 27 (Winter 2024). Kolkata, IN.

"Dream Screenshot." *Panoply: A Lit Zine*. Vol. 26 (Winter 2024).

"*Tercios del Muerte*." *Bulb Culture Collective Anthology*. Ed. L.M Cole and Jared Povanda. Spring 2024.

"Gas: Love Supreme." *The Croton Review*. Vol. 8. 1985.

"*Yo, Picasso*." Acceptance. *Eucalyptus Lit*. Vol. 3 (Spring 2024).

"Fogged." Voted Best of 2023 *Lit Shark Anthology*. Winter 2024; "Summertime, 2023." *Lit Shark*. Vol.5
   (Spring 2024).

 "Immersive"; "What Kandinsky Said"; "Klee to Kandinsky"; "Late"; "Too Late"; & "*Then*.
   COMP: An Interdisciplinary Journal. Vol. 3 (Spring 2024).

"*Blaue Blüme*." *The Rumen*. Spring 2024. (book retitled, "Immersive.")

"Private Eye" and "What Kandinsky Said." *Santa Clara Review*. Vol. 111. 2 (Summer 2024).

"Duchamp *Detourné*" and "Duchamp Kinetics." *Metachrosis Literary Magazine*. Vol. 4 (Summer 2024). Dundee,
   Scot. Both poems nominated for Best of Net Anthology Prize, 2024.

"*Au Rebours*," "Nightlight," "Sleepwalkers," "Wake," and "Gossamer Art." *Ginosko Literary
   Journal.*"Vol 32 (Summer 2024).

"Just Don't Call Me Ishmael." *Blue Feathers Anthology*. Vol. 5.2 (Summer 2024).

"Gossamer Art" and "Meadowlark, Walt, Me." *Reverie Magazine* (Autumn 2024); "Gossamer Art" rpt.
  Deer O Dear! Magazine. Vol. I (*Autumn* 2024).

 "AM" (now "(Y)am Man") and "Just Don't Call Me Ishmael." *Inkfish Magazine* (Autumn 2024). Cornwall, UK.

"Meadowlark, Walt, Me," winner of May-June Poem-of-the-Month. *Lit Shark: Shark Week Edition*, and
  "Nightlight." Vol. 7. *Shark Lit Magazine* (Autumn 2024), as well as in *Best of 2024 Anthology* (Winter 2025).

"*Au Rebours*." Vol 8. *Shark Lit Magazine* (Winter 2024).

"Blue Note," "I (*too!*) wander'd…," and "Reading the Signs." *Sweet Tea Dichotomy Literary Magazine*. Issue III.
  (Fall 2024).

"*In Lux Perpetua*" and "Total Eclipse." *Stone Poetry Quarterly* (Autumn 2024).

"*The Life*" and "Call It a Life." *Lit Shark Magazine*. Vol, 9 (Spring 2025).

"Raptured," "Dream of Vermeer," and "*In Lux Perpetua*." *Mikroksomos Journal*. Vol.7 (Spring 2025).

"Presence" and "Summertime, 2024." *Best of Lit Shark Magazine Anthology 2025*. Ed. McKenzie Lynn Tozan.
  (Spring 2025).

The Business of *Blue Business*

Blue Business articulates ways of seeing and reseeing predominately iconic classic, modern, and contemporary artists in contiguous forms who charted and shaped the grammar and content of paint and painting, poetry and music, their visual and visceral images and languages often in eclectic and eccentric aesthetics. Buson, Chagall, De Kooning, Duchamp, Ernst, Holiday, Hopper, Kandinsky, Klee, Matisse, Miró, Monet, O'Keeffe, Picasso, Pollock, Rothko, Van Gogh and Yung Shou-p'ing embody a tableaux of signature artists, along with personal, idiosyncratic artistic conceits in Section II. The *écriture*, textures and spatial architectonic of these "geometries of dancing dreams," "angles of notions," reconstruct the play and spirit of contemporaneity— of ink/oil/water/pastiche mediums. They illuminate art's implosive ambiguity, duplicity, insistent urge-to-order the unconscious: To reclaim in expressive abstraction, impression or *plein-air* chaos an all-of-a-moment comity. Since art insistently resists interpretation, paradigms of "critics and shrinks" and interpretive literary discourse, what sustains, after all, beyond the business of being blue, is "paint, painting, you."